CW01305467

"Florence Maybrick and Jack the Ripper"

By

Kieran James*
University of the West of Scotland
Kieran.James@uws.ac.uk and
Kieran.James99@yahoo.co.uk

A revised form of this article was originally published as follows: James, K. (2017), "The Florence Maybrick Trial of 1889 and the need for courts of criminal appeal", *International Journal of Critical Accounting*, Vol. 9, No. 2, pp. 85-102.

*Address for Correspondence: Dr Kieran James, School of Business and Enterprise, University of the West of Scotland, Paisley campus, Paisley, Renfrewshire, Scotland PA1 2BE, tel: +44 (0)141 848 3350, e-mail: Kieran.James@uws.ac.uk and Kieran.James99@yahoo.co.uk
Facebook: https://www.facebook.com/kieran.james.94

© Copyright Kieran James 2017, Paisley, Renfrewshire, Scotland

Published by Kieran James, 2017

ISBN 978-0-244-93877-2 (deluxe hardcover version)

ISBN 978-0-244-03891-5 (paperback version)

Author bio

Dr Kieran James is a Senior Lecturer in Accounting at the University of the West of Scotland, Paisley, Renfrewshire, Scotland. He was formerly the Accounting Professor at University of Fiji, Fiji Islands, from 2013-15. He has published scholarly articles in the following journals: *Accounting Forum*, *Critical Perspectives on Accounting*, *International Journal of Critical Accounting*, *International Journal of Social Economics*, *International Journal of Sport Management and Marketing*, *Musicology Australia*, *Pacific Accounting Review*, *Punk & Post Punk*, and *Sporting Traditions*. He runs a heavy-metal music website Busuk Chronicles which has had over 70,000 page-views as at 26 August 2017. He also founded and is the current manager of the Joo Chiat Road Online (Singapore politics); Nadi Legends Club (football); and WAFL Golden Era (Australian Rules football) websites.

Florence Maybrick and Jack the Ripper
Abstract

The criminal trial of Mrs Florence Maybrick, held in Liverpool, England during the height of the British Empire 1889, is widely regarded as one of the greatest travesties of justice in British legal history where even the judge at the end of the trial remarked "well, they can't convict her on that evidence" and the chief prosecutor nodded his head in agreement. Mrs Maybrick was tried for murdering her husband via arsenic poisoning. However, the trial became a morality trial when the learned judge, **Mr Justice James Fitzjames Stephen,** linked Mrs Maybrick's demonstrated adultery to her alleged desire to physically remove her husband by administering poison. The jury, which pronounced a guilty verdict, consisted of twelve untrained and unschooled men who were unable to grasp the technical evidence and were probably unduly influenced by the judge's summing-up and by the professional status of one of the medical witnesses for the prosecution. The case is a timely reminder today for an international audience of the fallibility and inherent weaknesses of the legal system and the desperate need to retain Courts of Criminal Appeal within the courts system.

Keywords: *Arsenic addiction*; *British History*; *Florence Maybrick*; *Legal History*; *Liverpool*; *Jack the Ripper*; *James Maybrick*; *Social History*.

Introduction

The criminal trial of Mrs Florence Maybrick, held in Liverpool, England during the height of the British Empire 1889, is widely regarded as one of the greatest travesties of justice in British legal history where even the judge at the end of the trial remarked "well, they can't convict her on that evidence" and the chief prosecutor nodded his head in agreement (as witnessed by a newspaper reporter and cited in Christie, 1968, p. 141). Mrs Maybrick was tried for murdering her husband via arsenic poisoning. However, the trial became a morality trial when the learned judge, **Mr Justice James Fitzjames Stephen,** linked Mrs Maybrick's demonstrated adultery to her alleged desire to physically remove her husband by administering poison. Mr Justice Stephen was wrong to attempt to, in the words of his brother Sir Leslie, turn his own criminal court into a "school of morality" (cited in Christie, 1968, p. 134). The jury, which pronounced a guilty verdict, consisted of twelve untrained and unschooled men who were unable to grasp the technical evidence and were probably unduly influenced by the judge's summing-up and by the professional status of one of the medical witnesses for the prosecution.

István Szijártó (2002, p. 212) writes that the advantages of microhistory such as the present paper are as follows: "…it can appeal to its readers by being interesting, it transmits lived experience, it stands on both feet on the ground of reality, and with all the lines branching out from the event, person or community in focus, it points towards the general". The case presented here is a timely reminder today for an international audience of the fallibility and inherent weaknesses of the legal system and the desperate need to retain Courts of Criminal Appeal within the courts system. It also suggests that senior judges aged over 55 years, and especially those who have suffered strokes or head injuries, need to be regularly evaluated by their peers or by other qualified persons. Mental decline can occur earlier than expected and can have disastrous consequences.

James and Florence Maybrick – the initial meeting and early married life

Mr James Maybrick, cotton merchant of Liverpool, was an eligible bachelor in his early-40s when he met the 17-year-old American Miss Florence "Florie" Elizabeth Chandler on board the steamer *SS Baltic* heading back from the USA to England which had departed from New York City on 11 March 1880 (Christie, 1968, p. 36; Feldman, 2007, pp. 75-6; Graham and Emmas, 1999, p. 28; Harrison, 2008, p. 219). Whilst gathered around the bar on the first evening offshore, Mr Maybrick was introduced by General J.G. Hazard of New Orleans to the Baroness von Roques and her daughter Florence (Christie, 1968, p. 37; Graham and Emmas, 1999, p. 28).[1] Mr Maybrick had been in the New World to attend to his cotton interests. Maybrick & Co. had opened an American office in the cotton-exporting port-city of Norfolk, Virginia in the late-1870s (Graham and Emmas, 1999, p. 31). Christie (1968, p. 37) was not over-exaggerating his point when he wrote that the introduction of James to Florence by General Hazard "set in motion a portentous train of events". To the surprise of many observers, James and Florence began a romance which had crystallized into a committed relationship by the time the ship arrived in Liverpool six days after its departure. When they left the ship it was decided that if they still felt the same way about

---

[1] The population of Norfolk had been 21,966 in 1880, rising to 34,871 ten years later.

each other in a year's time they would marry (Graham and Emmas, 1999, p. 32).² This criteria must have been fulfilled because the couple duly wed in St. James's Church (which still stands today) in London's Piccadilly on 27 July 1881 when Florence was only 18-years-old (Christie, 1968, p. 38; Feldman, 2007, p. 76; Graham and Emmas, 1999, p. 34; Maybrick, 2012, p. 21). Christie (1968, p. 39) offers the following observations about the marriage which seemed to begin favourably but soon deteriorated amidst adultery and arsenic addiction:

> "As events unfolded it is now clear that the marriage was founded in part on avarice and deception. While unquestionably sincere in his affections [how can Christie, from the vantage point of 1968, be so sure about this point?], James was intrigued by the Baroness's glib tales of a vast tract of Southern lands that would some day be inherited by her daughter. The mother, for her part, was nearing the end of her financial rope and envisioned a life of ease in her twilight years with the aid of a seemingly rich son-in-law. Genuinely in love for the first time [how can Christie, from the vantage point of 1968, be so sure about this point also?], Florie was an innocent pawn in the game – dominated by her mother, bedazzled by her bridegroom".

After briefly honeymooning in Bournemouth they lived in Norfolk for the next three years, spending about half their time in USA and the other half in Liverpool (Christie, 1968, p. 40). In 1884, James Maybrick was replaced by his brother Edwin as the buying agent for Maybrick & Co. in Norfolk, and James Maybrick's family returned to Liverpool (Christie, 1968, p. 40; Graham and Emmas, 1999, pp. 38-9). They first rented a house

---

² However, Nigel Morland (1957), incorrectly it seems, dates the first meeting of the couple to a trip from the USA to England in 1881 not 1880. This is why he, also incorrectly, assumes that the marriage occurred almost immediately after disembarking the ship.

known as Beechville in the suburb of Grassendale Park North (Christie, 1968, p. 40; Graham and Emmas, 1999, p. 39). The family later took out a five-year lease on Battlecrease House in Aigburth, near the Mersey River, Liverpool, in February 1888 (Graham and Emmas, 1999, pp. 43-4). According to Christie (1968, p. 41), and there can be no dissenting opinions here, "it was [at Battlecrease House] that fate would strike". The couple brought with them to the ill-fated Battlecrease House (which still stands today on Riversdale Road) their two children the elder Master James Chandler Maybrick ("Bobo") (born 24 March 1882) (Christie, 1968, p. 41; Graham and Emmas, 1999, p. 39, note; Maybrick, 2012, p. 21) and the younger Miss Gladys Evelyn Maybrick (born 20 June 1886, according to Maybrick, 2012, p. 21, and 21 June 1886, according to Graham and Emmas, 1999, p. 39).

Christie (1968, p. 42) comments that "[i]n an age dedicated to the worship of property and material things it is significant that Maybrick, despite his high position in the world of trade, never owned a home throughout his married life". The Maybricks were much like the "new money" Forsytes (although the Forsytes were richer than the Maybricks) in the novel *The Forsyte Saga*, always being concerned with the maintenance of the appearances befitting a family of high social standing. As Christie (1968, p. 42) commented: "From all appearances in the first years of their marriage the Maybricks were safely embarked on the conventional social life of Victorian England". An important reason for the Maybricks' endless whirl of dinner-parties was no doubt to impress their business and social acquaintances. Mr Maybrick's attitude towards his arsenic eating reflected the hypocrisies of the times, with him swinging from boasting about it to angrily denying it depending on the person he was talking to and the immediate context. For example, when Florie wrote to James' younger brother Michael in March 1889 to advise him that James was taking a "white powder" which might explain the pains in his head, James angrily responded to Michael's questioning about the powder with: "Whoever told you that? It is a damned lie" (cited in Christie 1968, pp. 48-9).

Mr and Mrs Maybrick's marital relationship worsened during their time at Battlecrease House when it was put under considerable strain by Mr Maybrick's financial problems, his arsenic habits, his infidelity (Edwards, 2007, p. 54), his aloofness, the couple's spending habits, and Mrs Maybrick's personal debts. Sometime during 1887 Florie discovered that James was regularly seeing and maintaining a mistress and it was from this point onwards that the Maybricks slept in separate beds (Christie, 1968, p. 45).

Mr Maybrick almost certainly had an arsenic addiction; the eating of arsenic by middle-class men as a medicinal or sexual tonic seems to have been a 19th century phenomenon. A brief, signed by Charles Russell QC, I. Fletcher Moulton QC, Harry Bookin Poland QC, and Reginald Smith QC, at Lincoln's Inn on 12 April 1892, and prepared by Messrs. Lumley & Lumley presents evidence that a Mr Valentine Charles Blake signed a statutory declaration to the effect that he had procured for Mr Maybrick 150 grains of arsenic around two months before his (Maybrick's) death (cited in Maybrick, 2012, pp. 278, footnote, pp. 312-3). Mary Howard of Norfolk, Virginia, the madam of a brothel Mr Maybrick patronized at least three times a week for several years prior to his marriage, spoke as follows about Mr Maybrick's arsenic eating: "I saw him frequently in his different moods and fancies". He took arsenic two or three times each evening, she swore, and she was afraid that he would die on the premises and "some of us [the house girls] would be suspected of his murder" (cited in Christie, 1968, p. 36). Thomas Stansell, a black servant of Maybrick's from his bachelor days in Norfolk (1878-80), also testified to Maybrick's arsenic habit but it seems that this witness failed to receive the respect he deserved in court perhaps for race-related reasons. Stansell testified that, in his first year of service, he was asked three or four times to go the drug-store and buy arsenic for Maybrick without a prescription (Christie, 1968, p. 119).

Mr Maybrick's health progressively deteriorated in late April 1889 and his death on 11 May 1889 of exhaustion caused by gastro-enteritis (**Graham and Emmas, 1999, p. 173**; Lumley

& Lumley-prepared brief cited in Maybrick, 2012, pp. 268, 309, 335) could have been influenced by the effects of arsenic withdrawal. The quantity of arsenic found in his body post-mortem, one-tenth of a grain total in the liver, kidney, and intestines, was consistent with an arsenic eater who had left off the habit for some time perhaps even for a couple of months (Christie, 1968, p. 70; Feldman, 1997; Lumley & Lumley-prepared brief cited in Maybrick, 2012, p. 336). The gastro-enteritis which killed Mr Maybrick was probably caused by bad food or drink or by excessive consumption of the same or by Mr Maybrick's distressing experience of being soaked wet on the day of the Wirral Races, 27 April 1889 (**Graham and Emmas, 1999, p. 173**; Lumley & Lumley-prepared brief cited in Maybrick, 2012, pp. 266, 268, 309). The effects of arsenic withdrawal may well have been a factor in his death (Christie, 1968, p. 167). In fact, Christie (1968, p. 167) calls this the "most sensible theory" yet advanced about the cause of death.

Key participants at the Florence Maybrick trial

For the first nine decades of the 20th century James and Florence Maybrick were remembered because of the notorious 1889 criminal trial of the American Florence when she was convicted of murdering her older English husband James by arsenic poisoning (Schoettler, 1993). During the trial the jury and court reflected on the salacious details of her affair with Alfred Brierley and the trial was widely regarded as a trial of Mrs Maybrick's morality. Consistent with the ethos of Victorian times Mr Maybrick's extra-marital relationships (Edwards, 2007, p. 54) were glossed over while those of his wife's were viewed as unforgivable (Christie, 1968, pp. 126-7; Graham and Emmas, 1999, p. 7). It was easy for many people of the era to believe that a woman capable of committing adultery was easily capable of committing murder as well. In fact, the aging Mr Justice James Fitzjames Stephen (born 3 March 1829 – died 11 March 1894) (father of "Jack-the-Ripper" serial-murder suspect James Kenneth Stephen, 25 February 1859 – 3 February 1892) presented the case to the jury specifically as a *morality trial* (as we shall see). Generally it is perceived that the defence erred in not asking for the trial to be moved away from Liverpool (Graham and Emmas, 1999, p. 156), as Mrs Maybrick had requested in a letter to her mother from Walton Jail (dated 28 June 1889) (Maybrick, 2012, p. 51). However, Mrs Maybrick herself suggested in her 1904 book *My Fifteen Lost Years* that the reason had been a funding shortfall (Graham and Emmas, 1999, pp. 157-8; Maybrick, 2012, p. 51).

Charles Russell (10 November 1832 – 10 August 1900) (later Baron Russell of Killowen and Lord Chief Justice of England) was Mrs Maybrick's famed defence lawyer and a strong supporter of her innocence (although at the time this was denied by certain commentators belonging to the anti-Florence Maybrick camp including Lord Hugh Cecil (Maybrick, 2012, pp. 144, 255)). Christie (1968, p. 72) remarks that Sir Charles: "was regarded by most authorities as the most brilliant advocate of his day". Confirming this assertion, he rose to the pinnacle of the English legal system, the Lord Chief Justice of England. However, Sir Charles performed only moderately well in defence of Mrs Maybrick. The reason for this was that he was mentally exhausted following his important role in the earlier Parnell Commission hearings which had included his finest hour, a six-day defence speech (Christie, 1968, p. 111; Graham and Emmas, 1999, p. 161). His biographer R. Barry O'Brien (1901, p. 259) wrote that: "To dwell on any of Russell's cases after the Parnell Commission would be an anti-climax" but he does spend five pages at this juncture on the Maybrick trial. Mrs Maybrick was later to call Sir Charles, who visited her in Aylesbury Prison, "the noblest, truest friend that woman ever had"; "the champion of the weak and the oppressed"; and "the brave upholder of justice and law in the face of prejudice and public hostility" (Maybrick, 2012, pp. 143-4). Sir Charles' direct opponent at the Florence Maybrick trial was Mr John Edmund Wentworth Addison QC MP (5 November 1838 – 22 April 1907).

Mr Justice Stephen exhibited signs of approaching insanity during the trial and he was widely regarded as being only a shadow of his former self (Graham and Emmas, 1999, p. 193; Maybrick, 2012, pp. 237, 393). He was forced to resign in April 1891 (Christie, 1968, p. 145; Graham and Emmas, 1999, p. 193; Maybrick, 2012, p. 393) and he died on 11 March 1894 in a private lunatic asylum in Ipswich (so clearly Mrs Maybrick (2012, p. 237) was wrong when she wrote in 1904 that he died "a year" after her trial) (Christie, 1968, p. 145; Graham and Emmas, 1999, p. 193). He was called "the great mad judge" in the Liverpool *Daily Post* of 13 August 1900 (cited in Maybrick, 2012, p. 238). This *Daily Post* article concluded that "[i]t was shocking to think that a human life depended upon the direction of this wreck of what was once a great judge" (cited in Maybrick, 2012, p. 239). In the 1890 second edition of his book *A General View of the Criminal Law of England* Mr Justice Stephen was to write that the Florence Maybrick case was the only case out of the 979 he had tried between January 1885 and September 1889 where "there could be any doubt about the facts" (Stephen, 1890, p. 174, cited in Christie, 1968, p. 145 and Maybrick, 2012, p. 394).

Mr Justice Stephen's closing address in the Florence Maybrick trial was an oddity in that he was favourable to Mrs Maybrick on the first afternoon but inexplicably changed his tone when he began again the next morning (Christie, 1968, pp. 19, 137; Graham and Emmas, 1999, p. 5; Lumley & Lumley-prepared brief cited in Maybrick, 2012, p. 364; Maybrick, 2012, p. 393). It was the closing day section of Mr Justice Stephen's address which was ultimately the one factor which was crucial in the failure of Sir Charles to secure his client's acquittal (Edwards, 2007, p. 54). Ultimately Mrs Maybrick was found guilty based on nothing more than "the mere gossip of servants" (Maybrick, 2012, p. 41). Christie (1968, pp. 56, 57) concludes as follows about the shadowy coalition below-stairs who were waiting for Mrs Maybrick to trip up so that they might conspire to do her harm:

> "It is undoubtedly true, however, that an amorphous, loosely organized cabal was operating at Battlecrease House to snare Florie in some misdeed that would break up her marriage and deprive her of her children; but, whatever its objective, it was certainly not to hound her to the gallows. ... Over the span of fifteen days from Saturday, April 27th [1889] to Saturday May 11th, this deadly cabal did its work at Battlecrease House".

Christie (1968, p. 56) lists Mrs Briggs, "abetted by her married and unmarried sisters", a group of women who had earlier held romantic aspirations in relation to both James and Alfred Brierley but who had remained friends of the family and were frequent visitors to Battlecrease. The aptly-named Miss Alice Yapp was also named by Christie, a nosy domestic-servant who opened a letter of Mrs Maybrick's she had been given for the purpose of posting it to Brierley on the pretext that three-year-old Gladys had dropped it in the mud. Alice Yapp was arguably bitter after suffering a recent relationship breakup of her own. Miss Yap brought the letter to Edwin Maybrick who telegraphed his brother Michael with instructions to come to the house straight away from London (Christie 1968, p. 61). Miss Yapp was also the one who reported to Mrs Briggs seeing flypapers in the bathroom and these were later tested for arsenic. In a recent murder trial in Liverpool two working-class women had been convicted for murder by obtaining arsenic from flypaper. On the same day as the two previously mentioned events, Miss Yap telegraphed Michael Maybrick with the message: "Come at once strange things going on here" (cited in Christie 1968, p. 61).

Drs Carter and Humphreys were ready and willing to write out "acute inflammation of the stomach" on the death certificate but only decided not to do so after a discussion with Michael where Mrs Maybrick was implicated (Christie, 1968, pp. 70, 99-101). We then had the strange situation of a musical composer advising two medical practitioners as to the cause of death (letter from family friend Charles Ratcliff to John Aunspaugh, May / June 1889, cited in Christie, 1968, pp. 63-4). After the cross-examination of Dr Humphreys at the trial, Christie (1968, p. 100) remarks that "[t]here were strong doubts [among those assembled in the courtroom] as to how far Michael Maybrick and his suspicions had swayed the doctor in withholding a certificate of death". At Michael's insistence, James' body was exhumed two weeks after its burial but, as mentioned earlier, only one-tenth of a grain was found in the kidney, liver, and intestines and none in the rest of the body (Christie, 1968, p. 70).

My analysis of the Florence Maybrick trial

Mrs Maybrick was found guilty largely based on the flypaper containing arsenic (Edwards, 2007, p. 54). She claimed that she was using this recipe as a facial treatment (Schoettler, 1993). Lumley & Lumley noted that: "[t]he purchase and soaking of fly-papers is the only direct evidence of the possession of arsenic in any form by Mrs. Maybrick" (cited in Maybrick, 2012, p. 269). After she was imprisoned her mother found such a fly-paper recipe dated 1878 inside Mrs Maybrick's family Bible, which was cited by the Lumley & Lumley-prepared brief (cited in Maybrick, 2012, pp. 347-8) as additional evidence in favour of her innocence. This prescription for face-wash containing arsenic was signed by a Dr Bay of New York City (Christie, 1968, pp. 216-7; Maybrick, 2012, p. 348). It was duly made up by a French chemist in Paris on 17 July 1878 (Christie, 1968, pp. 216-7; Maybrick, 2012, p. 348). Unfortunately this information was received far too late for the original trial and the authorities consistently rejected appeals for a new trial. Other evidence unfavourable to Florence included: the finding of arsenic in meat juice (half a grain); on a handkerchief; on a dressing-gown; in a bottle; and in a package labelled "Arsenic: Poison for Cats" (Christie, 1968, p. 102). The handkerchief; dressing-gown; bottle; and package were all found in the defendant's bedroom (Christie, 1968, p. 102). The amounts ranged from a fraction of a grain to 65 grains (Christie, 1968, p. 102), but are also consistent with self-medication of arsenic by James. The ridiculous inscription on the package "Arsenic: Poison for Cats" strongly suggests a sick joke and possible malicious intent on the part of the domestic servants.

The following somewhat strange statement by the Home Secretary, Mr Henry Matthews (13 January 1826 - 3 April 1913), was the ground for the 1889 decision to spare Mrs Maybrick the death penalty and reduce her sentence to life imprisonment:

> "After the fullest consideration, and after taking the best medical and legal advice that could be obtained, the Home Secretary [H.M.] advised Her Majesty [Queen Victoria] to respite the capital punishment of Florence Elizabeth Maybrick and to commute the punishment to penal servitude for life; inasmuch as, although the evidence leads to the conclusion that the prisoner administered and attempted to administer arsenic to her husband with intent to murder him, yet it does not wholly exclude a reasonable doubt *whether his death was in fact caused by the administration of arsenic*" [cited in Maybrick, 2012, pp. 226-7, emphasis original].

As Maybrick (2012) explains, there are a number of major problems raised by this statement. Firstly, if there was indeed "reasonable doubt" (a legal term) whether James Maybrick's death *"was in fact caused by the administration of arsenic"* then the prisoner Mrs Maybrick should have been found "not guilty" by the jury and should have been immediately set free rather than simply have had her sentence reduced to life imprisonment (Henry W. Lucy, *The Strand Magazine*, London, November 1900, cited in Maybrick, 2012, p. 253). Henry Matthews was indeed trying to claim some totally untenable middle ground. For the jury to have found Mrs Maybrick guilty, all of the following pre-conditions should have been satisfied: (a) that Mr Maybrick's death was caused by arsenic poisoning; (b) that Mrs Maybrick administered the fatal dose of arsenic; and (c) that the arsenic was administered by Mrs Maybrick with the intent to kill (Christie, 1968, p. 113).

If only pre-conditions (a) and (b) were present then Mrs Maybrick could have been convicted on a lesser charge but not on the charge of murder. In fact, there were serious doubts associated with each of the three necessary pre-conditions and it can well be argued that none of the three pre-conditions, even taken as individual propositions, were ever proved beyond reasonable doubt. In regards pre-condition (a), taken by itself, if over 65 grains of arsenic was found in the house how can we explain why such a tiny quantity of arsenic was found in the body of the deceased? Even if the Home Office's statement that "although the evidence leads to the conclusion that the prisoner administered and attempted to administer arsenic to her husband with intent to murder him" was valid (which it wasn't (Lumley & Lumley-prepared brief cited in Maybrick, 2012, p. 296)) this should not have been enough to have sustained a murder charge because the death had not been proven beyond reasonable doubt to have been caused by arsenic poisoning (Maybrick, 2012, p. 244). Even Mr Justice Stephen, although on the whole a poor performer at the trial, had told the members of the jury that "[i]t is *essential* to this charge *that the man died of arsenic*" (cited in Maybrick, 2012, p. 227, emphasis original).

Secondly, Mrs Maybrick was never tried at court for "administering and attempting to administer arsenic ... with intent to murder" her husband (Lumley & Lumley-prepared brief cited in Maybrick, 2012, p. 365) so she could not and should not have been found guilty of such a charge (Christie, 1968, p. 170; Maybrick, 2012, p. 228). This was the charge which the Home Office perhaps wished or imagined that Mrs Maybrick had been charged with.

The medical evidence made it clear that the quantity of arsenic contained in Mr Maybrick's body – one-tenth of a grain – was insufficient to have caused death (Maybrick, 2012, p. 235; Lumley & Lumley-prepared brief cited in Maybrick, 2012, pp. 313-4). Mr Davies found 0.02 of a grain in the liver and Dr Stevenson found 0.076 of a grain in the liver and 0.015 in the intestines making the total amount found by both doctors combined around one-tenth of a grain (Graham and Emmas, 1999, p. 173; Lumley & Lumley-prepared brief cited in Maybrick, 2012, p. 311). The smallest quantity of arsenic previously found to have caused a victim's death had been two grains and this was with respect to a woman who had not been an arsenic eater during life (Lumley & Lumley-prepared brief cited in Maybrick, 2012, p. 311). The experienced doctors for the defence (Dr Stevenson excepted) were of the opinion that the low quantity of arsenic found in Mr Maybrick's body was consistent with "administration in medicinal doses, and [the arsenic] might have been introduced a considerable time before [death]" (Maybrick, 2012, p. 235 and see also Lumley & Lumley-prepared brief cited in Maybrick, 2012, p. 313). In other words, the evidence merely showed that Mr Maybrick had been self-administering arsenic and that he may have stopped doing so (with disastrous consequences) some time prior to his eventual demise.

We should now briefly refer to the sub-standard responses from the star expert witness for the prosecution, Dr Thomas Stevenson (a lecturer on forensic medicine and chemistry at Guy's Hospital (Christie, 1968, p. 107)), under cross-examination in the courtroom. The evidence also shows how deeply divided the doctors on this case were. In response to a question from QC Addison for the prosecution, the witness answered as follows: "I have no doubts that this man died from the effects of arsenic" (cited in Christie, 1968, p. 108). It is worth following the cross-examination responses closely. When he was then asked about the fatal dose of arsenic needed to kill an adult he responded: "Two grains or thereabouts" (cited in Christie, 1968, p. 108). Then it was Sir Charles' turn to cross-examine. Christie (1986, p. 109) remarks that: "Sir Charles realized he had a formidable witness on his hands", but the reference to "formidable" should be held to refer to his overall self-confident presence rather than to the quality of his answers. Sir Charles asked whether there is any "distinct symptom" of arsenic poisoning which distinguishes it from gastroenteritis caused by other factors. Dr Stevenson was snide and over-confident when he replied: "There is no distinctive diagnostic symptom of arsenical poisoning: the diagnostic thing is finding the arsenic". We see here the doctor falling into the careful trap laid by the expert defence counsel. Sir Charles let his case rest when he then got Dr Stevenson to confess that 0.076 of a grain of arsenic was found in the liver and 0.015 of a grain in the intestines, totalling 0.091 of a grain. Clearly then, given that "*the diagnostic thing is finding the arsenic*", there was no evidence at all that Mr Maybrick died from arsenic poisoning. As Christie (1968, p. 110) concludes: "If two grains of the poison is a fatal dose on the average, as the witness had testified, it is not surprising that many in the court felt that such minute traces of arsenic represented rather feeble evidence on which to base the doctor's opinion as to the cause of death". Sir Charles could be forgiven if he believed that this time he had landed the case's decisive blow. In contrast to the testimony of Dr Stevenson, Dr Charles Tidy of the London Hospital (who held a position comparable to Dr Stevenson's at Guy's (Christie, 1968, p. 115)) and Dr Frank T. Paul, medical authority at University College, Liverpool and Victoria University, Manchester, both argued that it was *not* a case of arsenic poisoning; Dr Tidy said the case "absolutely points away from arsenic as the cause of death" while Dr Paul testified that "[t]he post-mortem appearances do not show that it was set up by arsenic" (cited in Christie, 1968, p. 117).

On the second and concluding day of his summing-up, Mr Justice Stephen told the jury as follows:

> "You must consider the case as *a mere medical case*, in which you are to decide whether the man did or did not die of arsenic according to the medical evidence. You must not consider it as *a mere chemical case*, in which you decide whether the man died from arsenic which was discovered as the result of a chemical analysis. You must decide it *as a great, high, and important case*, involving in itself not only medical and chemical questions, but embodying in itself *a most highly important moral question* – and by that term, moral question, I do not mean a question of what is right and wrong in a moral point of view, but questions in which human nature enters and in which *you must rely on your knowledge of human nature* in determining the resolution you arrive at.
>
> "I could say a good many other things about the awful nature of the charge, but I do not think it will be necessary to do any one thing. Your own hearts must tell you what it is for a person *to go on administering poison* to a helpless, sick man, upon whom she has already inflicted a dreadful injury – an injury fatal to married life; the person who could do such a thing as that must be destitute of the least trace of human feeling. ... We have to consider this not in an unfeeling spirit – far from it – but in the spirit of people resolved to solve *by intellectual means an intellectual problem of great difficulty* [cited in Maybrick, 2012, pp. 319-21, emphasis original].

This extraordinarily incoherent, muddled, and problematic set of statements, which was very influential in determining Mrs Maybrick's eventual fate, deserves careful study. In the first sentence the statement appears to begin well but it immediately deteriorates in quality from that point onwards, and doubles back to contradict itself. Instead of the above incoherent statements, the judge instead should have asked the jurors to reflect upon three straight-forward questions and three straight-forward questions only (Lumley & Lumley-prepared brief cited in Maybrick, 2012, p. 321): (a) did Mr Maybrick die of arsenic poisoning; (b) did Mrs Maybrick administer arsenic to Mr Maybrick; and (c) did she do so with the intent to kill? Mr Justice Stephen's last-quoted statement that the members of the jury must "solve *by intellectual means an intellectual problem of great difficulty*" (emphasis original) seems faintly ridiculous given that the medical evidence clearly indicated that Mr Maybrick's body contained around one-tenth of a grain of arsenic and the smallest quantity ever known to have killed someone was two grains (or twenty times as much). It hardly seems an intellectual feat of staggering proportions for someone to conclude that there was reasonable doubt that Mr Maybrick did *not* die of arsenic poisoning.

What is especially interesting in Mr Justice Stephen's statements is that he directly informed the uneducated laymen of the jury to disregard the expert medical testimony of the experienced doctors for the defence including Dr Tidy and Dr Paul. This is the interpretation which I give to the following sentence: "You must not consider it as *a mere chemical case*, in which you decide whether the man died from arsenic which was discovered as the result of a chemical analysis" (emphasis original). When this sentence is taken out of the convoluted paragraph in which it first appears its inappropriateness is even starker. Instead of giving due weight to the medical evidence, Mr Justice Stephen instead referred the members of the jury to *"a most highly important moral question"* (emphasis original) where they must *"rely on your [their] knowledge of human nature"*. In other words, Mr Justice Stephen set this case up *as a trial of the morality of Mrs Maybrick*. He then stated that "she has already inflicted a dreadful injury – an injury fatal to married life" upon Mr Maybrick. He was thus explicitly encouraging the jurors to regard Mrs Maybrick's adultery and her husband's strange death while she was nursing him as connected sordid pieces of the same morality play. The adultery was specifically portrayed as relevant. By encouraging the jurors to *"rely on your [their] knowledge of human nature"* (emphasis original) Mr Justice Stephen appeared to be implying that the "human nature" of someone who had inflicted the injury of adultery upon her husband would incline that same person to want to remove her husband's presence physically so as to begin a new life with her lover. However, Mr. Justice Stephen ignored the facts that the Brierley affair had long since ended and that Mrs Maybrick could simply have divorced her husband and in fact had already taken some steps in that direction (Maybrick, 2012, p. 365). QC Addison, on behalf of the prosecution, had earlier set the deadly wheels in motion when he had (reprehensibly) claimed that Mrs

Maybrick "had so interwoven her adultery with her conduct that it was impossible to treat it as an ordinary case of adultery and not treat it as having any actual connection with the alleged crime" (cited in Christie, 1968, p. 131).

Mr Justice Stephen was clearly on a dangerous course when he instructed the jurors to listen to "[y]our [their] own hearts [which] must tell you [them] what it is for a person *to go on administering poison* to a helpless, sick man, upon whom she has already inflicted a dreadful injury" (emphasis original). Given that it was an all-male jury (Graham and Emmas, 1999) (women jurors were first used in England in 1920) the appeal for them to effectively listen to their emotions was clearly inflammatory and most prejudicial to Mrs Maybrick's cause. Mr Justice Stephen was effectively asking the jurors to put themselves in Mr Maybrick's shoes, imagine that it was their wives who had betrayed them personally, and then to feel the full gamut of emotions which such circumstances would engender. Clearly, in such a context, a man's own adultery would not be relevant and Mr Justice Stephen in the above quoted statements did not refer to it. Mrs Maybrick (2012, p. 236) wrote that "[t]he jury belonged to a class of men who were not competent to weigh technical evidence", and so direct pleas by Mr Justice Stephen to the emotions of the jurors would most likely have been powerfully effective.[3] Despite the case

---

[3] The jury consisted of three plumbers, two farmers, one milliner, one wood-turner, one provision dealer, one grocer, one ironmonger, one house-painter, and one baker (Christie, 1968, p. 79; Graham and Emmas, 1999, p. 164; Maybrick, 2012, p. 236 footnote).

producing nearly 800,000 words of testimony it took the jurors only 38 minutes to reach their guilty verdict (Christie, 1968, p. 20). Another basic factual error made by Mr Justice Stephen was to say "you have been convicted by a jury of this city" (cited in Christie, 1968, p. 20). The jury members were from Lancashire County but not from the city of Liverpool. One of the judge's more serious factual errors, which even the Crown counsel was forced to correct him on, was to state that the reconciliation between husband and wife had taken place before (rather than after) Florence's overnight tryst with Brierley at Flatman's Hotel in London (Christie, 1968, p. 139).

Lastly, there was no evidence presented at the trial which conclusively proved that Mrs Maybrick had administered arsenic or any other poison to her late husband, and Mr Justice Stephen clearly erred by suggesting that such evidence had been presented. The statement "the person who could do such a thing as that must be destitute of the least trace of human feeling" clearly suggests a morality trial where the judge had already found the prisoner guilty before the jurors had even left the courtroom to begin their deliberations. It seems that Mrs Maybrick was found guilty by the judge of harbouring a certain state of alleged inner wickedness rather than because of actual proven actions or actual physical evidence. There is also an obvious ambiguity in that the judge's statement that "the person who could do such a thing as that" could reasonably be held to be referring back to *either* the adultery of Mrs Maybrick or to her alleged administration of poison to her late husband. The ambiguity suggests that both the adultery and the alleged administration of poison were both seen by the judge as consistent with and indicative of the certain state of alleged wickedness which I claim the judge was imputing to Mrs Maybrick. Mr Justice Stephen's brother Sir Leslie, in his biography of his brother, remarked that James (Stephen) was a "moralist in the old-fashioned sense" and that "he took advantage of his strength to carry out his own ideals of a criminal court as a school of morality" (cited in Christie, 1968, p. 134).

Mr Justice Stephen also mentioned a dog that had apparently died of arsenic poisoning, although there was no trace of arsenic in its body post-mortem, either not realizing or not caring that arsenic would work its way through a dog's system much quicker than it would a man's (Lumley & Lumley-prepared brief cited in Maybrick, 2012, p. 323). The judge turned himself into an impromptu witness for the prosecution during his closing address; his ill-advised statements were of such a nature that any defence lawyer would have torn them to shreds. However, Sir Charles was not given this opportunity. The judge at the end of the trial remarked: "well, they can't convict her on that evidence" and the chief prosecutor, QC Addison, nodded his head to agree (as allegedly witnessed by a newspaper reporter and cited in Christie, 1968, p. 141). At the end of the trial Sir Charles was overheard saying to his fellow barristers in the corridors of St. George's Hall: "Mark what I say, it is the most dangerous verdict that has ever been recorded in my experience" (cited in Graham and Emmas, 1999, p. 9). Within half an hour of the trial ending, a petition against the verdict was signed by every junior barrister and by every Queen's Counsel present at the Assize Courts that day (Graham and Emmas, 1999, p. 9).

Although many informed commentators at the time, including Sir Charles, and afterwards suggested that Mrs Maybrick had been wrongly convicted (Beadle, 2005a; Maybrick, 2012, p. 225) there was no Court of Criminal Appeal at that time. Mrs Maybrick (2012, p. 89) wrote in 1904 that "[t]he supineness of Parliament in not establishing a court of criminal appeal fastens a dark blot upon the judicature of England, and is inconsistent with the innate love of justice and fair play of its people". Other notable advocates for a Court of Criminal Appeal were Lord Esher in *The Times* of 17 August 1889 and *The Times* newspaper itself of the same date (Maybrick, 2012, p. 260). A Court of Criminal Appeal was eventually established by the *Criminal Appeal Act 1907* (Christie, 1968, p. 266). The Florence Maybrick case is a timely reminder today for an international audience of the fallibility and inherent weaknesses of the legal system and the desperate need to retain Courts of Criminal Appeal within the courts system.

Later life of Mrs Maybrick

As mentioned, Mrs Maybrick's death sentence was nearly immediately reduced to life imprisonment on the directions of the Home Office (Adamson, 1993, p. 6; Edwards, 2007, p. 54; Maybrick, 2012, p. 60; O'Brien, 1901, p. 259). Sir Charles continued to lobby the Home Office for Florence's release up until his death in 1900. As O'Brien (1901, p. 263) wrote: "And so, to the end, the fate of this unhappy woman occupied his thoughts, and he never ceased, either in private or officially, to say that there had been a grave miscarriage of justice in the case, and that Florence Maybrick "ought to be allowed to go free"'. Mrs Maybrick was transferred from Woking Prison to Aylesbury Prison on 4 November 1896 (Christie, 1968, p. 181; Maybrick, 2012, pp. 127-32) when the former institution was reassigned to be used for military purposes (Maybrick, 2012, p. 132). In the end she was released after having served just fifteen years (Beadle, 2005a; Edwards, 2007, p. 54). At the date of her departure she was the only prisoner left at Aylesbury Prison who had also been a prisoner at Woking Prison (Maybrick, 2012, p. 194). However, her final release was not a special dispensation (Maybrick, 2012, p. 251) but was the result of a review which was accorded to all "life" prisoners after 20 years or somewhere between 15 and 20 years when there had been good behaviour (Maybrick, 2012, p. 211). It does appear that Queen Victoria had an ill opinion of Mrs Maybrick and, because of this, Mrs Maybrick's release was only possible after the Queen's death on 22 January 1901. The Queen had convicted Mrs Maybrick for immorality in her own mind and was hostile to reversing that decision (Christie, 1968, pp. 224-5). This was finally confirmed as proven fact in 1930 when George Earle Buckle published an edition of the Queen's letters (Christie, 1968, p. 224).

Mrs Maybrick was 41-years-old when she was released at 6.45am on Monday 25 January 1904 (Christie, 1968, p. 227; Maybrick, 2012, p. 217). She spent the last six months of her sentence recuperating at Home of the Community of the Epiphany in Truro, Cornwall, from which she was released on 20 July 1904 (Maybrick, 2012, p. 218-9). About her time spent in Truro, Florence commented: "I look back upon the six months spent within those sacred walls as the most peaceful and happiest – in the true sense – of my life". After staying with her devoted mother in Rouen, France for three weeks (Maybrick, 2012, pp. 11, 220), Mrs Maybrick boarded the Red Star Line steamship *Vaderland* at Antwerp, Belgium bound for New York City (Christie, 1968, p. 229; Maybrick, 2012, p. 221) and "the sacred soil of my [her] native land" (Maybrick, 2012, p. 222). Her name was entered on the ship's passenger list as Rose Ingraham "that I [she] might secure more quiet and privacy" (Maybrick, 2012, p. 221). The ship arrived in New York

Harbour on 23 August 1904 (Christie, 1968, p. 230; Maybrick, 2012, p. 222).

After being an itinerant speaker about prison conditions for some years, Mrs Maybrick passed away on 23 October 1941 (Adamson, 1993, p. 6). She never remarried. For over a decade before her death she had been living as a recluse with her cats in the rolling hills of the Connecticut countryside near Gaylordsville, South Kent (Christie, 1968, Chapter 15). She was described by Colin Adamson in *The Evening Standard* newspaper (now renamed *The London Evening Standard*) of 22 April 1993 as having "died penniless and in squalor in America" (Adamson, 1993, p. 6). She had befriended the local school staff and was a well-known local eccentric in the community and at the school. Mrs Maybrick never again got to see her own children ("the children to whom I am dead" (Maybrick, 2012, p. 223)), Bobo and Gladys, after they were forcibly removed from her, at the orders of Mr Maybrick's domineering younger brother Michael (Graham and Emmas, 1999, p. 125; Maybrick, 2012, p. 25), in May 1889 (Maybrick, 2012, pp. 25, 223 footnote). According to Michael Maybrick, Bobo, who had been made acquainted with the anti-Florence Maybrick version of his mother's trial, "did not wish either his own or his sister's photograph to be sent to me [Florence]" in prison which up until then had been the annual practice (Maybrick, 2012, p. 223 footnote). For a family which was apparently never too far removed from tragedy, it is perhaps not surprising that Bobo was killed in a bizarre mining accident in Canada in April 1911, aged 29, when he drank a tube of cyanide believing it to be water (Christie, 1968, pp. 245-6). He left his sister Gladys a sizeable estate of £4,755 (Christie, 1968, p. 246). For her part, Gladys married in 1912 and died in South Wales in 1971 aged 85.

With very little supporting evidence Paul Feldman (2007, pp. 181-3) concludes that Florence had an illegitimate son, William Graham (Billy Graham's father / author Anne Graham's grandfather), born in Hartlepool, England in January 1879 when she was 16-years-old (see also Beadle, 2005a; Graham and Emmas, 1999, p. xxi). Feldman (2007) surmises that this child's existence explains why Florence hoped to see "them" (plural) (*Sunday News*, 1 May 1927, cited in Feldman, 2007, pp. 181-2), meaning "her children" (plural), in a last visit to England in 1927 when she already knew that her son Bobo had died in the 1911 mining accident and Gladys was her only other child with James (Feldman, 2007, p. 183).

Recent developments: the "Jack-the-Ripper" diary

The discovery of the alleged "Jack the Ripper" diary was made in May 1991 (Beadle, 2005a; Begg, 2005, p. 369; Skinner, 1999, p. x), when a Liverpudlian unemployed scrap-metal merchant Michael Barrett was allegedly handed the diary by his drinking friend the late Tony Devereux **(Whitehead and Rivett, 2012, p. 124)**, a retired printer (Knightley, 1993; **Schoettler, 1993**), in **Liverpool** pub The Saddle Inn[4] (Begg, 2005, p. 369; Knightley, 1993). The diary (hereafter referred to as "the Diary") claims internally to be authored by the 19th century Liverpool cotton merchant James Maybrick (25 October 1838 – 11 May 1889) (Adamson, 1993, p. 6; Edwards, 2007, p. 54; Gowers, 1995; Harrison, 2008, p. 215; Skinner, 1999, p. x) and also to be the diary of the never apprehended Whitechapel serial-killer "Jack the Ripper" of 1888 (Adamson, 1993, p. 6; Beadle, 2005a; Edwards, 2007, p. 54; Feldman, 2007; Harrison, 2008, p. 215; Knightley, 1993; Linder et al., 2003; **Schoettler, 1993**).

Noted Jack the Ripper author Keith Skinner (1999, p. ix) writes that: "The alleged 'Diary of Jack the Ripper' has always been shrouded in controversy, ever since it first came into the public domain back in 1992". Before the discovery of the Diary, which has somewhat dubious "provenance" (Beadle, 2005b; Begg, 2005, p. 369; George, 2006; Knightley, 1993), no writer on the Jack the Ripper murders of 1888 had ever nominated

---

[4] This Saddle Inn (located at 86 Fountains Road) is about equidistant from Anfield and Goodison Park football stadiums and should not be confused with The Saddle Inn at 13 Dale Street (in the Liverpool city-centre).

James Maybrick as a plausible suspect (Harrison, 2008, p. 214; May, 2007).[5] It was the internal Diary references to "Battlecrease House", in Riversdale Road, Liverpool, which led Michael Barrett, in his follow-up private research, to conclude that the Diary's author was clearly presenting himself to the world as being James Maybrick (Harrison, 2008, p. 214).

Tony May (2007) from Hastings, East Sussex comments as follows: "He [Maybrick] was not connected to the enquiry at the time, and had not even been thought of as a suspect until the diary came to light so, in fairness to him, [i]f we believe the diary to be a fake I think we should all acknowledge his innocence". However, despite voluminous debate amongst Ripperologists (students of the Jack the Ripper murders) over the past 20 years and numerous forensic tests of ink, phraseology, and hand-writing, the possibility that the Diary is in fact genuine has not been conclusively disproved (Edwards, 2007, p. 54; George, 2007).[6] Christopher T. George (2007), the Editor of *Ripperologist* magazine, writes as follows: "the Diary has not been conclusively proven to be a hoax because no one

---

[5] I use the term "Jack the Ripper murders" rather than the more genteel "Whitechapel murders" not to shock but because the latter term includes all murders committed in the Whitechapel region during the period 1888-91 which were not obviously domestics or gangland killings. These include the "torso murders" which experts agree are unlikely to be by the same hand as the murders committed by the serial killer Jack the Ripper (Evans and Skinner, 2000, p. 480; Rumbelow, 2013, p. 135). The Jack the Ripper murders are generally thought to include: Mary Ann "Polly" Nichols, Annie Chapman; Elizabeth Stride; Catharine Eddowes; and Mary Jane Kelly (all 1888); as well as possibly Martha "Maggie" Tabram (1888); Alice MacKenzie (1889); and Frances Coles (1891).

[6] For space reasons I forego in this paper any extended discussion of the debates about the Diary's authenticity. Interested readers are referred to the debates for and against the Diary on the Yoliverpool.com forum at: http://www.yoliverpool.com/forum/showthread.php?2439-James-Maybrick [accessed 18 June 2013].

has been proven conclusively to have forged it". The fact that forgery has not been proven (Harrison, 2008, p. 230) is itself significant given that the "Hitler diaries", for which the *Sunday Times* paid £1 million in 1983 (Schoettler, 1993), were exposed as fraudulent within a relatively short space of time (Knightley, 1993; Schoettler, 1993). In fact, a leading history professor has stated that the Diary is "probably genuine" or it would have been proven to be a forgery by now. Harrison (2008, p. 230) observes that: "[The Diary] has survived possibly the most rigorous investigation of any manuscript this [twentieth] century".

A more satisfactory provenance was later given the Diary when Michael Barrett's ex-wife Anne Graham claimed that her late father Billy had been bequeathed the Diary among the possessions of his grandmother Elizabeth Formby (Beadle, 2005a) before World War II; had first seen it when he came home on leave from the army in 1943; and had finally taken possession of it in 1950 (Begg, 2005, p. 371). Ms Graham gave the Diary to Tony Devereux, so that he would give it to her then husband Barrett. Ms Graham was hoping that her then unemployed husband would use it to write a novel; she did not give it to him personally because she was worried he would bother her aging father with endless questions about it (Beadle, 2005a; Begg, 2005, p. 372). If this story is to be believed it points in favour of the Diary's authenticity since there are facts in the Diary which were not made public until 1987 (Knightley, 1993). It follows unarguably, from the internal text of the Diary, that James Maybrick and Jack the Ripper are one and the same person (Harrison, 2008, p. 215). Given the fact that forgery has *not* been proven (Harrison, 2008, p. 230), it is certainly not impossible that it is in fact a genuine document. The possible origins of the Diary are as follows: (a) it is a modern forgery; (b) it is an old forgery written for unknown reasons but perhaps to benefit Florence during the trial; (c) it was written by James Maybrick but the events described are pure fantasy; and (d) James Maybrick really was Jack the Ripper.

According to the Diary, Mrs Maybrick's infidelity (the Diary refers to her as "the whore" and "the whoring mother" (Beadle, 2005a; Graham and Emmas, 1999, p. 64)) in turn led her husband James into a period of mental anguish (mixed with sexual excitement (Begg, 2005, p. 370; Graham and Emmas, 1999, p. 71)). This prolonged intense emotional state then led to the series of Jack the Ripper murders where the casual prostitutes of the East End of London literally stood in as "scapegoat[s]" (Graham and Emmas, 1999, p. 53) for the "whoring" Florence.

My concluding comments about the Diary are as follows: The Jack-the-Ripper Diary, incriminating James Maybrick, is an interesting modern development which has not yet been conclusively proven or disproven although it is regarded as suspect by most Jack-the-Ripper scholars. If the Diary's internal claim is valid, James Maybrick confessed his crimes to his wife prior to his death but this was not mentioned in court for fear that it would grant Florence an additional "motive" for murder. However, the importance of the Florence Maybrick case today in no way stands or falls on the validity of the Diary. For one hundred years the Jack-the-Ripper case and the Florence Maybrick poison case were linked only by their closeness in time.

Conclusion

The criminal trial of Mrs Florence Maybrick, held in Liverpool, England during the height of the British Empire 1889, is widely regarded as one of the greatest travesties of justice in British legal history where even the judge at the end of the trial remarked "well, they can't convict her on that evidence" and the chief prosecutor nodded his head in agreement. Mrs Maybrick was tried for murdering her husband via arsenic poisoning. However, the trial became a morality trial when the presiding judge, **Mr Justice Stephen,** linked Mrs Maybrick's demonstrated adultery to her alleged desire to physically remove her husband by administering poison. Mr Justice Stephen was wrong to attempt to, in the words of his brother Sir Leslie, turn his own criminal court into a "school of morality". The Jack-the-Ripper Diary, incriminating James Maybrick, is an interesting modern development which has not yet been conclusively proven or disproven. However, the importance of the Florence Maybrick case today in no way stands or falls on the validity of the Diary.

Szijártó (2002, p. 211, emphasis added) writes that microhistory can usefully, when "contextualiz[ed] as full[y] as possible, put the stress on the *ramifications* of *the single case*". The Florence Maybrick trial of 1889 remains today a timely reminder for an international audience of the fallibility and inherent weaknesses of the legal system and the desperate need to retain Courts of Criminal Appeal within the courts system. Following Szijártó (2002, p. 211), "[we must] step beyond the individual case and proceed towards the general". I was lecturing in the Fiji Islands at the time this paper was written (2013-2015). It is fortunate that Fiji has a Court of Appeal enshrined in the new 2013 *Constitution*[7] (Section 99(1)-(5), Government of Fiji, 2013, p. 57). However, I humbly suggest that there should be a splitting up of this court into a Court of Criminal Appeal and a Court of Appeal for civil (non-criminal) cases. The Maybrick case also suggests that senior judges aged over 55 years, and especially those who have suffered strokes or head injuries, need to be regularly evaluated by their peers or by other qualified persons. Mental decline can occur earlier than expected and can have devastating consequences. The Maybrick case also highlights the weakness of the English jury system where uneducated people are asked to pass judgement on what must appear to them to be complex medical evidence. Christie (1968, pp. 78-9) commented that the jurors lacked "the technical training to cope with the complex medical and legal testimony". In the Florence Maybrick trial the jurors were overly impressed by the bearing, reputation, and social standing of the judge and of the star medical practitioner witness, Dr Stevenson, who testified in a manner prejudicial to the interests of the accused.

---

[7] This *Constitution* was issued by the government of Frank Bainimarama in September 2013 prior to the 2014 General Election which was won by his Fiji First party.

References

Adamson, Colin (1993), "Is this the face of Jack the Ripper?" *Evening Standard [UK]*, 22 April, p. 6.

Beadle, William (2005a), "Revisiting the *Maybrick 'Diary'* – Part One", available online at: http://www.jamesmaybrick.org/pdf%20files/Diary%20(William%20Beadle%20article).pdf [accessed 18 June 2013].

Beadle, William (2005b), "Revisiting the *Maybrick 'Diary'* – Part Two", available online at: http://www.jamesmaybrick.org/pdf%20files/Diary%20(William%20Beadle%20article).pdf [accessed 18 June 2013].

Begg, Paul (2005), *Jack the Ripper: the Definitive History*, revised paperback edition (Harlow: Pearson Education).

Christie, Trevor L. (1968), *Etched in Arsenic* (Philadelphia, PA: Philadelphia Lippincott).

Edwards, Martin (2007), *Mind to Kill* (Hoo, Kent: Grange Books).

Evans, Stewart P. and Skinner, Keith (2000), *The Ultimate Jack the Ripper Sourcebook: An Illustrated Encyclopedia* (London: Constable and Robinson).

Feldman, Paul (2007), *Jack the Ripper: the Final Chapter*, paperback edition (London: Virgin Books).

George, Christopher T. (2006), "Untitled forum post", Yoliverpool.com, 11 August, available online at http://www.yoliverpool.com/forum/showthread.php?2439-James-Maybrick, [accessed 26 June 2013].

George, Christopher T. (2007), "Untitled forum post", Yoliverpool.com, 2 May, available online at http://www.yoliverpool.com/forum/showthread.php?2439-James-Maybrick/page3, [accessed 26 June 2013].

Government of Fiji (2013), *Constitution of the Republic of Fiji*, available online at: http://www.paclii.org/fj/Fiji-Constitution-English-2013.pdf [accessed 24 June 2016].

Gowers, Rebecca (1995), "At each others' throats over Jack the Ripper", 31 August, *The Independent [UK]*, available online at: http://www.independent.co.uk/news/at-each-others-throats-over-jack-the-ripper-1598714.html [accessed 28 August 2013].

Graham, Anne E. and Emmas, Carol (1999), *The Last Victim: the Extraordinary Life of Florence Maybrick, the Wife of Jack the Ripper* (London: Headline Book Publishing).

Harrison, Shirley (2008). "The Diary of Jack the Ripper", in: M. Jakubowski and N. Braund (eds.), *The Mammoth Book of Jack the Ripper*, American edition (Philadelphia, PA: Running Press Book Publishers), pp. 213-236.

Knightley, Phillip (1993), "Is this man Jack the Ripper?: Certainly a lot of money is being spent trying to tell you so", *The Independent [UK]*, 29 August, available online at: http://www.independent.co.uk/news/uk/is-this-man-jack-the-ripper-certainly-a-lot-of-money-is-being-spent-trying-to-tell-you-so-phillip-knightley-a-veteran-of-publishing-hoaxes-untangles-the-evidence--and-feels-he-has-been-here-before-1464073.html [accessed 14 June 2013]

Linder, Seth, Morris, Caroline and Skinner, Keith (2003), *Ripper Diary: the Inside Story* (London: Sutton Publishing).

May, Tony (2007), "Untitled forum post", Yoliverpool.com, 2 November, available online at http://www.yoliverpool.com/forum/showthread.php?2439-James-Maybrick/page4, [accessed 26 June 2013].

Maybrick, Florence (2012), *Mrs. Maybrick's Own Story: My Fifteen Lost Years* (New York, NY: Forgotten Books) [originally published 1904].

Morland, Nigel (1957), *This Friendless Lady* (London: Frederick Muller).

O'Brien, R. Barry (1901), *Life of Lord Russell of Killowen* (London: Smith, Elder and Co).

Rumbelow, Donald (2013), *The Complete Jack the Ripper: Fully Revised and Updated* (London: Virgin Books).

Schoettler, Carl (1993), "The Ripper's 'diary,' not yet published, is being slashed to pieces", *The Baltimore Sun [USA]*, 23 September, available online at: http://articles.baltimoresun.com/1993-09-23/features/1993266235_1_jack-the-ripper-diary-gryphon [accessed 18 June 2013].

Skinner, Keith (1999), "Foreword", in *The Last Victim: The Extraordinary Life of Florence Maybrick, the Wife of Jack the Ripper* (London: Headline Book Publishing), pp. ix-xv.

Stephen, James F. (1890), *A General View of the Criminal Law of England*, 2nd edition (London and New York, NY: Macmillan) [reproduced from the original copy held at Harvard Law School Library as part of the *Gale Making of the Modern Law: Legal Treatises, 1800-1926* series].

Szijártó, István (2002), "Four Arguments for Microhistory", *Rethinking History*, Vol. 6, No. 2, pp. 209-215.

Whitehead, Mark and Rivett, Miriam (2012), *Jack the Ripper* (Harpenden, Hertfordshire: Pocket Essentials).

www.ingramcontent.com/pod-product-compliance
Ingram Content Group UK Ltd.
Pitfield, Milton Keynes, MK11 3LW, UK
UKHW021313180725
6961UKWH00003B/20